1B

FOUR CORNERS

Second Edition   Workbook

JACK C. RICHARDS & DAVID BOHLKE

CAMBRIDGE
UNIVERSITY PRESS

CAMBRIDGE
UNIVERSITY PRESS

University Printing House, Cambridge CB2 8BS, United Kingdom

One Liberty Plaza, 20th Floor, New York, NY 10006, USA

477 Williamstown Road, Port Melbourne, VIC 3207, Australia

314–321, 3rd Floor, Plot 3, Splendor Forum, Jasola District Centre, New Delhi – 110025, India

79 Anson Road, #06–04/06, Singapore 079906

Cambridge University Press is part of the University of Cambridge.

It furthers the University's mission by disseminating knowledge in the pursuit of education, learning and research at the highest international levels of excellence.

www.cambridge.org
Information on this title: www.cambridge.org/fourcorners

© Cambridge University Press 2012, 2019

First published 2012
Second edition 2019

20 19 18 17 16 15 14 13 12 11 10 9 8 7 6 5 4 3 2

Printed in Malaysia by Vivar Printing

A catalogue record for this publication is available from the British Library

ISBN 978-1-108-65961-1   Student's Book with Online Self-Study 1
ISBN 978-1-108-68741-6   Student's Book with Online Self-Study 1A
ISBN 978-1-108-64936-0   Student's Book with Online Self-Study 1B
ISBN 978-1-108-56045-0   Student's Book with Online Self-Study and Online Workbook 1
ISBN 978-1-108-56048-1   Student's Book with Online Self-Study and Online Workbook 1A
ISBN 978-1-108-56399-4   Student's Book with Online Self-Study and Online Workbook 1B
ISBN 978-1-108-45950-1   Workbook 1
ISBN 978-1-108-45953-2   Workbook 1A
ISBN 978-1-108-45955-6   Workbook 1B
ISBN 978-1-108-63367-3   Teacher's Edition with Complete Assessment Program 1
ISBN 978-1-108-64464-8   Full Contact with Online Self-Study 1
ISBN 978-1-108-59712-8   Full Contact with Online Self-Study 1A
ISBN 978-1-316-99950-9   Full Contact with Online Self-Study 1B
ISBN 978-1-108-45973-0   Presentation Plus Level 1

Additional resources for this publication at www.cambridge.org/fourcorners

Contents

Credits

The authors and publishers acknowledge the following sources of copyright material and are grateful for the permissions granted. While every effort has been made, it has not always been possible to identify the sources of all the material used, or to trace all copyright holders. If any omissions are brought to our notice, we will be happy to include the appropriate acknowledgements on reprinting and in the next update to the digital edition, as applicable.

Photography
The following photographs are sourced from Getty Images:
U7: Tpopova/iStock; Robyn Mackenzie; Maya13/iStock; Mg7/iStock; Salma_lx/iStock; Andriscam/iStock; Andrea Chu/DigitalVision; **U8:** Adam Mork/ArcaidImages; Andrew Hetherington/Stone; Irfan Khan/Los Angeles Times; Alan Danaher/The Image Bank; **U9:** SnowWhiteimages/iStock; Purestock; **U10:** Gary John Norman/The Image Bank; Stockbyte; Mike Powell/The Image Bank; **U11:** James Woodson/Photodisc; Jochen Conrad/EyeEm; Monkey Business Images; Pando Hall/Photographer's Choice RF; Ariel Skelley/DigitalVision; Todd Arena/Thinkstock; Westend61; Jupiterimages/Stockbyte; **U12:** Comstock/Stockbyte; Drazen/E+.

The following photographs are sourced from other libraries:
U7: Piksel/Dreamstime.com; Elena Elisseeva/Shutterstock; Infografick/Shutterstock; Nattika/Shutterstock; Nattika/Shutterstock; Don Smetzer/Alamy Stock Photo; 3445128471/Shutterstock; Andrjuss/Shutterstock; Kiboka/Shutterstock; Cooddy/Shutterstock; UpperCut Images/Alamy Stock Photo; Serg Shalimoff/Shutterstock; **U8:** Ian Dagnall/Alamy Stock Photo; Alex Segre/Alamy Stock Photo; Frances Roberts/Alamy Stock Photo; Vespasian/Alamy Stock Photo; David R. Frazier Photolibrary, Inc./Alamy Stock Photo; Fancy/Media Bakery; David R. Frazier Photolibrary, Inc./Alamy Stock Photo; Kord/Media Bakery; Peter Titmuss/Alamy Stock Photo; **U9:** Age fotostock/Alamy Stock Photo; Directphoto Collection/Alamy Stock Photo; Lindy Powers/Alamy Stock Photo; **U10:** Heide Benser/Media Bakery; Paul Doyle/Alamy Stock Photo; Ei Katsumata - CMC/Alamy Stock Photo; William Manning/Alamy Stock Photo; **U11:** F1online; John Mitchell/Alamy Stock Photo; ImageBROKER/Alamy Stock Photo; James Godman/Media Bakery; Canva Pty Ltd/Alamy Stock Photo; Bill Bachmann/Alamy Stock Photo; Image Source Plus/Alamy Stock Photo; Eye Ubiquitous/Alamy Stock Photo; Carlos S. Pereyra/Media Bakery; Neil McAllister/Alamy Stock Photo; **U12:** Dario Sabljak/Shutterstock; Kedrov/Shutterstock; Patti McConville/Alamy Stock Photo; Le Do/Shutterstock; David Schaffer/Media Bakery; Lorraine Kourafas/Shutterstock; ShutterPNPhotography/Shutterstock.

Illustration
QBS Learning.

Front Cover by Sergio Mendoza Hochmann/Moment; Betsie Van der Meer/DigitalVision; andresr/E+.
Back Cover by Monty Rakusen/Cultura.

Food

A Breakfast, lunch, and dinner

1 Look at the pictures. Complete the puzzle with food words. What's the mystery word?

| ¹C | H | E | E | S | E |

2 Complete the sentences with the words from Exercise 1.

1 Lynn usually eats _____noodles_____ at her favorite Chinese restaurant.

2 I can't eat dairy. I never eat _____ .

3 Carl's favorite food is fruit. He eats _____ and _____
every day.

4 I usually have milk and fruit with my _____ in the morning.

5 _____ and _____ are my favorite vegetables.

6 Tanya's favorite grain is _____ . She usually has it with beans.

3 What food do you eat? Write two examples for each group or *I don't eat . . .*

Example: _I eat bananas and apples._ or _I don't eat fruit._

1 **Fruit:** _____

2 **Vegetables:** _____

3 **Meat:** _____

4 **Dairy:** _____

5 **Grains:** _____

4 Are the food words count or noncount nouns? Write C (count) or N (noncount).

1 apple _C_ 　　　3 milk _____ 　　　5 meat _____ 　　　7 chicken _____

2 cheese _____ 　　4 tomato _____ 　　6 pasta _____ 　　　8 egg _____

5 Complete the answers. Use *some* or *any*.

1 Do you have any carrots? 　　No, _I don't have any_____.

2 Do you have any fish? 　　　Yes, _____.

3 Do we have any apples? 　　Yes, _____.

4 Does Edward have any cereal? No, _____.

5 Do they have any beans? 　　No, _____.

6 Does Lorena have any rice? 　Yes, _____.

6 Complete the conversation with *a*, *an*, *any*, or *some*.

A What do you usually have for breakfast?

B I usually have ____some____ cereal.
　　　　　　　　　　　1

A Do you have _____ milk with it?
　　　　　　　　　2

B Yes, I do.

A And do you eat _____ fruit?
　　　　　　　　　　3

B Sometimes. I usually have _____ banana or
　　　　　　　　　　　　　　　4

_____ apple with my cereal.
　　5

A Do you eat _____ rice?
　　　　　　　　6

B Not for breakfast. But I sometimes have _____
　　　　　　　　　　　　　　　　　　　7

rice for lunch. I make it with _____ chicken or
　　　　　　　　　　　　　8

_____ beef and _____ vegetables.
　9　　　　　　　　10

Oh, and sometimes with _____ egg.
　　　　　　　　　　　　11

A Really?

B Yes. It's Korean food.

A And what about dinner? What do you usually eat?

B Well, I don't usually have _____ meat for dinner. I often have _____ pasta.
　　　　　　　　　　　　　12　　　　　　　　　　　　　　　　　13

It's my favorite!

50

7 Look at Andrea's food and her shopping list. What food does she have? What food doesn't she have? Write sentences with *some* and *any*.

Shopping List

apples
pasta
fish
beans
rice

1   Andrea has some tomatoes.
2   She doesn't have any apples.
3   _____
4   _____
5   _____
6   _____
7   _____
8   _____
9   _____
10 _____

8 Complete the lists with your own information. Then write sentences with *some* and *any*.

I have
_____
_____
_____
_____
_____

Shopping List

I don't have
_____
_____
_____
_____
_____

1   _____
2   _____
3   _____
4   _____
5   _____
6   _____

B I like Chinese food!

1 Complete the conversation. Use the correct forms of the expressions from the box.

love	really like	like	not like	not like at all	hate

Shelby Let's make lunch. Do you like noodles?

Martin No, I _don't like noodles_____ .
             1

Shelby How about Mexican food?

Martin Yes, I _____ .
                        2

Shelby OK. How about rice and beans?

Martin I _____ .
                       3

Shelby OK. Rice and beans. We have some fish, too.

Martin I _____ . How about chicken?
                       4

Shelby I _____ . How about beef?
                       5

Martin I _____ . Let's have rice and
                       6
beans with beef!

Shelby OK.

2 Complete the conversation with your own information. Use some of the expressions from Exercise 1.

Shelby Do you like fish?

You _____ , I _____ fish.

Shelby Do you like pasta?

You _____ .

Shelby How about eggs?

You _____ .

Shelby Do you like Chinese food?

You _____ .

Shelby How about Italian food?

You _____ .

C Meals

1 **Read the text. Then label the pictures with the correct underlined food words.**

Sometimes it's difficult to eat out with my friends. Everybody likes different kinds of food! My friend Jon loves Asian food. He likes <u>dumplings</u>, and he really likes <u>sushi</u>. Sandy usually eats pasta. She loves <u>spaghetti</u> and noodles. Jake, her brother, likes American food. He usually has a <u>hot dog</u> or a <u>hamburger</u>. Louis likes <u>tacos</u>, but his favorite meal is breakfast. He loves cereal, eggs, and <u>pancakes</u>. And Kristen is always on a diet. She only eats <u>soup</u> and <u>salad</u>. It's terrible! How about me? Well, I eat anything. I love all kinds of food!

1 ___hot dog___

2 _____

3 _____

4 _____

5 _____

6 _____

7 _____

8 _____

9 _____

2 Cross out the word that doesn't belong in each list.

1	**On pizza:**	tomatoes	cheese	~~pancakes~~
2	**Italian food:**	pizza	hot dogs	spaghetti
3	**In a salad:**	carrots	cheese	soup
4	**Japanese food:**	tacos	sushi	rice
5	**In soup:**	noodles	salad	chicken

3 Correct the mistakes.

1 Brenda eats every day pizza.   _Brenda eats pizza every day._

2 Ahmed eats tacos once year.   _____

3 We don't eat meat often very.   _____

4 Andy eats cheese two a month.   _____

5 Never Lydia eats vegetables.   _____

6 They have dumplings four a week.   _____

4 Circle the correct words to complete the conversation.

Pat How **once** / (**often**) do you eat sushi?
         1

Alan I don't eat sushi very **never** / **often**. How about you?
                                    2

Pat I eat sushi **once** / **twice** in a while. Kevin and I go to a
                      3
Japanese restaurant **twice** / **three** times a year.
                               4

Alan My family **every** / **never** eats out. We cook at home
                            5
every / **often** day.
        6

Pat Really? I don't cook **very** / **every** often. Kevin cooks
                                7
often / **twice** a week, but we usually go to
        8
restaurants.

5 Match the sentences that have similar meanings.

1 Gary eats spaghetti every Sunday. ___c___

2 Kyle doesn't eat spaghetti. _____

3 Marco eats spaghetti every Tuesday and Friday. _____

4 Mr. Lee eats spaghetti three times a year. _____

5 Victor has spaghetti once a month. _____

a He eats spaghetti once in a while.

b He eats spaghetti twice a week.

c He eats spaghetti once a week.

d He eats spaghetti 12 times a year.

e He never eats spaghetti.

6 Look at Karen's answers to the quiz. Then answer the questions.

How international is your diet?

How often do you have . . .	every day	twice a week	once a week	twice a month	once in a while	never
Brazilian food?			✓			
Colombian food?						✓
Japanese food?		✓				
Korean food?				✓		
American food?	✓					
Italian food?			✓			
Greek food?					✓	

1   How often does Karen eat Brazilian food?   *She eats Brazilian food once a week.*

2   How often does she eat Colombian food?   _____

3   How often does she eat Japanese food?   _____

4   How often does she eat Korean food?   _____

5   How often does she eat American food?   _____

6   How often does she eat Italian food?   _____

7   How often does she eat Greek food?   _____

7 How international is *your* diet? Answer the quiz with your own information.
Then write sentences with the time expressions.

How often do you have . . .	every day	twice a week	once a week	twice a month	once in a while	never
Mexican food?						
Peruvian food?						
Thai food?						
Chinese food?						
Turkish food?						
French food?						

Example: *I never eat Mexican food.*

1   _____   4   _____

2   _____   5   _____

3   _____   6   _____

D Favorite food

1 Look at the photo at the end of Exercise 2. What kind of food is it?

It's _____ .

2 Read the text. Then answer the questions.

1 How often does Isabel eat at a Chinese restaurant? _____

2 Who makes Mexican food? _____

3 What's Isabel's favorite recipe? _____

HOME   RECIPES   TIPS   BLOG   CONTACT

EASY CHEF FORUM

**What do you usually eat? How often do you eat out?
What's your favorite recipe? We want to hear from you!**

Isabel

In my family, we usually have a well-balanced diet. We eat vegetables, fruit, and grains every day. We eat chicken about three times a week, and we eat fish once or twice a week. We hardly ever have beef. We eat it once in a while at restaurants, but we don't eat out very often. We do have some special days, though. Once a month, we eat out with our children at our favorite Chinese restaurant. The dumplings are delicious! And my mom comes over and makes Mexican food twice a month.

Here's my favorite easy recipe:

Veggie Pizza

Get some Italian bread. Put vegetables on top.
I use peppers, tomatoes, and onions.
Then add cheese, and cook it in the microwave
for one minute. Delicious!

3 Read the text again. Then write T (true), F (false), or NI (no information).

1 Isabel has two children. __NI__

2 Isabel's family eats vegetables seven days a week. _____

3 Isabel's mother makes Mexican food for the family every week. _____

4 Isabel's husband sometimes makes veggie pizza. _____

5 Isabel's family never has beef. _____

6 Isabel can't cook Mexican food. _____

7 Isabel likes dumplings. _____

8 Peppers are vegetables. _____

In the neighborhood

A Around town

1 Label the pictures with the correct words from the box.

bank	coffee shop	newsstand
bookstore	gas station	subway station
bus stop	✓ library	supermarket

1 _____library_____

2 _____

3 _____

4 _____

5 _____

6 _____

7 _____

8 _____

9 _____

2 Answer the questions. Use the places from Exercise 1.

1 Where can you usually get some coffee? _____At a coffee shop, a bookstore, or a gas station._____

2 Where can you usually get a newspaper? _____

3 Where can you usually get a book? _____

4 Where can you get gas for a car? _____

5 Where can you usually get some food? _____

3 Look at the picture. Complete the sentences with the correct words from the box.

across from	between	in	next to	✓ on	on the corner of

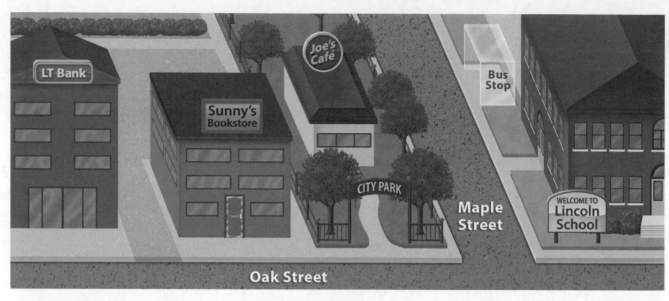

1 The bus stop is _____on_____ Maple Street.

2 The park is _____ Oak Street and Maple Street.

3 Joe's Café is _____ the park.

4 The bookstore is _____ the bank and the park.

5 The school is _____ the park.

6 The bank is _____ the bookstore.

4 Put the words in the correct order to make sentences. Sometimes more than one answer is possible.

1 is / The / supermarket / next to / the / post office / .

  The supermarket is next to the post office. / The post office is next to the supermarket.

2 The / Linden Street / department store / on / is / .

  _____

3 the / hotel / drugstore / across from / The / is / .

  _____

4 bookstore / café / in / the / The / is / .

  _____

5 the / library / The / bank and the school / is / between / .

  _____

6 First Avenue / The / hotel / is / on the corner of / and / Market Street / .

  _____

5 **Read the clues. Label the places with the correct words. Then answer the questions.**

A • The supermarket is on the corner of Second Avenue and Prince Street.

   • The coffee shop is between the bank and the hotel.

   • The library is next to the bank.

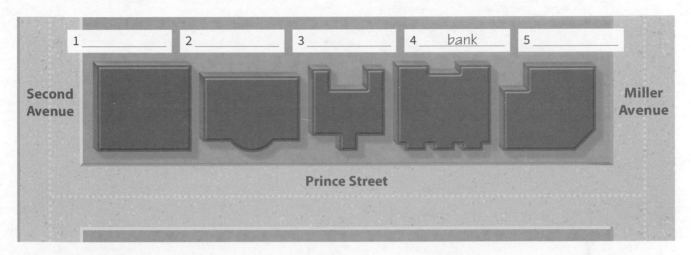

1 _____ 2 _____ 3 _____ 4 _bank_ 5 _____

Second Avenue **Miller Avenue**

Prince Street

1 Is the hotel between the coffee shop and the supermarket?   _Yes, it is._

2 What is on the corner of Miller Avenue and Prince Street?   _____

3 What is next to the supermarket?   _____

4 Is the coffee shop next to the library?   _____

B • The drugstore is across from the post office.

   • The police station is next to the drugstore.

   • The bookstore isn't on Oak Street.

   • The newsstand is next to the bookstore.

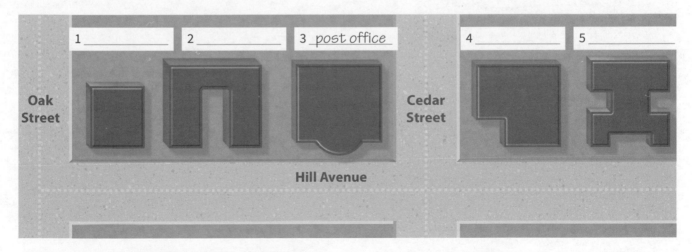

1 _____ 2 _____ 3 _post office_ 4 _____ 5 _____

Oak Street **Cedar Street**

Hill Avenue

1 What is on the corner of Oak Street and Hill Avenue?   _____

2 What is between the post office and the newsstand?   _____

3 Is the police station on Hill Avenue?   _____

4 Is the bookstore across from the drugstore?   _____

B How do I get to...?

1 Complete the directions with the correct words from the box.

| blocks | left | take | turn | up | ✓walk |

4:21PM

▶ **Start:** 150 York Street

● **End:** 45 East Eighth Street

▶ Start on York Street. _____Walk_____ to the corner of Elm Street.
1

▶ Take a _____ on Elm Street.
2

▶ Go _____ Elm Street.
3

▶ _____ right on Fifth Avenue.
4

▶ Walk four _____ .
5

▶ _____ a right on Eighth Street.
6

▶ Go down Eighth Street. It's on the left.

---

2 Write the conversation in the correct order.

✓ Excuse me. How do I get to the drugstore?
Go up Oak Street and turn left on First Avenue.
Great. Thank you very much.
Turn left on First Avenue?
Yes.

A   Excuse me. How do I get to the drugstore?
B   _____
A   _____
B   _____
A   _____

C Fun in the city

1 Complete the puzzle and the sentences with the correct places to visit.

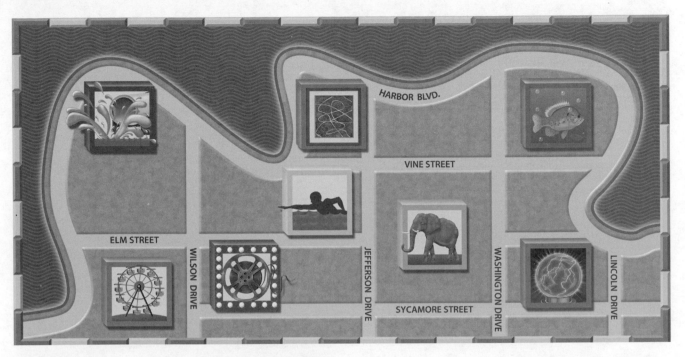

HARBOR BLVD.

VINE STREET

ELM STREET

WILSON DRIVE

JEFFERSON DRIVE

SYCAMORE STREET

WASHINGTON DRIVE

LINCOLN DRIVE

Across

2 Let's watch a movie at the _____ *movie* _____ theater.

3 My children can swim, and they love the _____ park.

5 Do you like the fish in the _____ ?

6 Is there a _____ pool here?

7 Don works at the science _____ .

Down

1 Let's see the animals at the _____ .

2 I really like the art at this _____ .

4 The _____ park is fun! Wheeeeeeee!

2 Read the text. Then answer the questions.

GATLINBURG, TENNESSEE

Welcome!

There's a lot to do in Gatlinburg! Read about all of the fun places to visit here!

Indoor fun

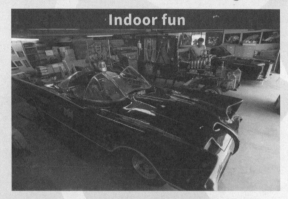

We have a lot of museums. Go to the Hollywood Star Cars Museum and see musicians' cars. You can see actors' and actresses' cars, too! Ripley's Believe It or Not Museum is also great. And Ripley's Aquarium has very unusual fish.

Outdoor fun

Great Smoky Mountains National Park is near Gatlinburg. It has 150 hiking trails! For other outdoor activities, you can try the alpine slide or water raft rides at Ober Gatlinburg Ski Area and Amusement Park.

1 Are there any museums in Gatlinburg? _Yes, there are._

2 Is there an aquarium in Gatlinburg? _____

3 Is there a national park near Gatlinburg? _____

4 Are there 200 hiking trails in the park? _____

5 Is there a ski area in Gatlinburg? _____

6 Is there an amusement park? _____

3 Write sentences about Gatlinburg with *there is / are / isn't / aren't* and the information in parentheses.

1 (aquariums / 1) _There's an aquarium in Gatlinburg._

2 (museums / 9) _____

3 (zoos / 0) _____

4 (movie theaters / 4) _____

5 (ski areas / 1) _____

6 (amusement parks / 1) _____

4 Complete the conversations. Use the correct forms of *there is* / *are*.

A Excuse me. <u>Are there any museums in this city</u> ?

 1

B _____ . The museums are on First
 2

Street.

A Great. And are there any zoos here?

B No, _____ , but there's an aquarium.
 3

It's near the art museum.

A OK. Thanks.

C Excuse me. _____ near here?
 4

D A swimming pool? Yes, _____ .
 5

_____ one in the park.
 6

C Great. _____ near the park?
 7

D No, _____ . The library is across from
 8

the school, about ten blocks from here.

C Thank you very much.

5 Complete the chart with the number of each place in your town or city.
Then write sentences with *there is* / *are* and the information in the chart.

Place	Number
amusement parks	
aquariums	
movie theaters	
museums	
science centers	
swimming pools	
zoos	

1 <u>There</u> _____ <u>in my town.</u>

2 _____

3 _____

4 _____

5 _____

6 _____

7 _____

D A great place to visit

1 Look at the calendar in Exercise 2. Is the Ridgewood Community Center open every day?

_____

2 Read the text. Complete the sentences with the correct days of the week.

1 You can see a movie at the community center on ____Friday____.

2 You can visit a museum on _____.

3 There's an Italian dinner at the community center on _____.

4 The swimming pool is open all day on _____.

5 There is a book sale on _____.

6 You can go to an amusement park on _____.

Ridgewood Community Center
Calendar

Monday	Tuesday	Wednesday	Thursday	Friday	Saturday
Children's Art Tour 2:30 – 4:30 p.m.	**Open Swim** All day	**Italian Night** 6:00 – 8:00 p.m.	**Bookstore** All day	**Movie Night** 6:00 – 10:00 p.m.	**Field Trip** 9:00 a.m. – 7:00 p.m.
Tour the new Metro Art Museum with two guides. This is for children age 6-12 and their parents.	Our swimming pool is open to everyone on Tuesday!	There's an Italian dinner at our community center. Come and eat spaghetti!	Bring old books to the center on Monday. On Thursday we have a book sale.	Watch a movie at the center. There's a drama in Room B, and there's a children's movie in Room D.	We take a bus to the Great Fun Amusement Park in Oakdale in the morning and come back in the evening.
$5 per person	_It's free!_	_$8 for adults_ _$6 for children_	_All books are $1._	_They're free!_	_$45 per person_

NOTE: _We are closed on Sundays._

Directions:

By bus: Take the Q62 bus to the Lamont bus stop. Walk down Lamont Street. Turn left on Orchid Street. We're on the corner of Orchid Street and Main Street.

By subway: Take the C train to Melvin Station. Walk up the stairs and turn right on View Street. Walk to Main Street and turn right. Walk two blocks to the corner of Main Street and Orchid Street.

3 Read the text again. Then answer the questions.

1 How much is the museum tour?   It's five dollars per person._____

2 What time is the Italian dinner?   _____

3 Is there a swimming pool at the community center? _____

4 How do they get to the amusement park? _____

5 Where is the community center in Ridgewood? _____

64

What are you doing?

A I'm looking for you.

1 Complete the sentences with the correct words from the box.

at	behind	front	in	in	on	✓ to	to	under

a He waves __to__ Paula. She is _____ the children.

b He runs _____ the movie theater.

c Bob is _____ the bus. He's late.

d She stands _____ an umbrella in the rain.

e Paula stands in _____ of the movie theater.

f The movie ends _____ 5:00.

g She looks for Bob _____ the lobby.

h The movie starts, but Paula isn't _____ the theater.

2 Match the pictures and the sentences from Exercise 1.

1 ☐ e

2 ☐

3 ☐

4 ☐

5 ☐

6 ☐

7 ☐

8 ☐

3 **Circle the correct words to complete each sentence.**

1 Calvin _____ at the bus stop.
  a are standing
  (b) is standing
  c stand

2 Kate and Naomi _____ to Jen.
  a aren't waving
  b isn't waving
  c don't waving

3 We _____ to our parents.
  a talks
  b don't talking
  c aren't talking

4 _____ starting now.
  a It's
  b It doesn't
  c It

5 _____ walking to school.
  a I'm not
  b I don't
  c I

6 Lori and Ross _____ behind Jay.
  a is sitting
  b sits
  c are sitting

4 **Rewrite the email to correct the underlined mistakes.**

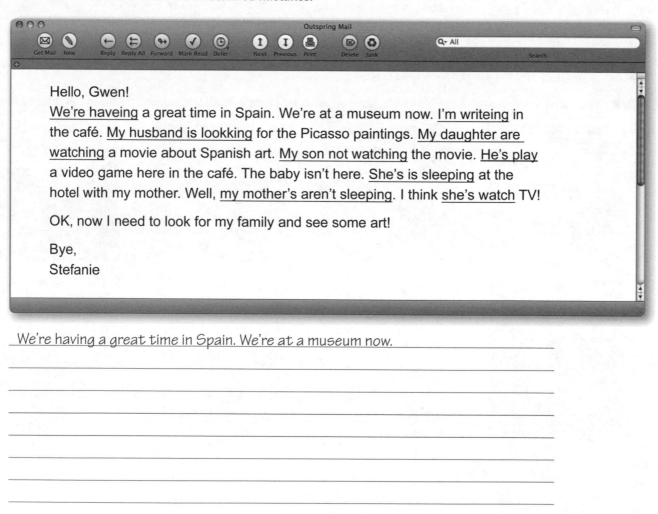

Hello, Gwen!
We're haveing a great time in Spain. We're at a museum now. I'm writeing in the café. My husband is lookking for the Picasso paintings. My daughter are watching a movie about Spanish art. My son not watching the movie. He's play a video game here in the café. The baby isn't here. She's is sleeping at the hotel with my mother. Well, my mother's aren't sleeping. I think she's watch TV!

OK, now I need to look for my family and see some art!

Bye,
Stefanie

  We're having a great time in Spain. We're at a museum now.
  _____
  _____
  _____
  _____
  _____
  _____
  _____

5 Write present continuous sentences with the words in parentheses.

1 (Matt / not drive / to work)   <u>Matt is not driving to work.</u>
2 (We / play / soccer / at the park)   _____
3 (Chloe / not sit / in the café)   _____
4 (The game / start / now)   _____
5 (They / swim / in the pool)   _____
6 (Joan / not have / lunch right now)   _____
7 (I / call / Audrey)   _____
8 (You / not run)   _____

6 Look at the pictures. What are the people doing? What aren't they doing? Complete the two sentences for each picture with the pairs of expressions from the box. Use the present continuous.

cook / eat at a restaurant	look for a book / hold a book
end / start	✓ run / watch a movie

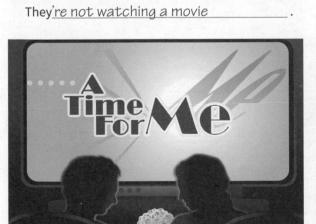 

1 They<u>'re running</u>_____ .
   They<u>'re not watching a movie</u>____ .

2 She _____ .
   She _____ .

3 The movie _____ .
   It _____ .

4 He _____ .
   He _____ .

B I can't talk right now.

1 Circle the correct words to complete each sentence.

Sally Hello?

Jordan Hi, Sal. It's Jordan. Do you have **good time** / (**a minute**)?
$_1$

Sally Oh, **sure** / **sorry**. I'm **busy** / **can't** right now. I'm cleaning.
$_2$ $_3$
Can I **call** / **talk** you back?
$_4$

Jordan OK, **sure** / **sorry**. Talk to you **minute** / **later**.
$_5$ $_6$

Sally Thanks. Bye.

2 Look at the pictures. Write conversations with the sentences from the box. Use the conversation in Exercise 1 as a model. Sometimes more than one answer is possible.

Can you talk now?	I'm cooking dinner.	Is this a good time to talk?
I can't talk right now.	I'm doing my homework.	This isn't a good time.

A. **Jin Sun** Hello?

   Ivan Hi, Jin Sun. It's Ivan.

   _____?

   Jin Sun _____ . _____ .

   _____ . _____?

   Ivan _____ . _____ .

   Jin Sun _____ . _____ .

B. **Dan** _____?

   Marc _____ . _____ .

   _____?

   Dan _____ . _____ .

   _____ . _____?

   Marc _____ . _____ .

   Dan _____ . _____ .

C These days

1 Put the letters in the correct order to make activity phrases.

1 erlan ot evdri   <u>learn to drive</u>

2 keat a cedan sslac _____

3 eecatr a stbeiew _____

4 oklo fro a bjo _____

5 tsudy tlilana _____

6 rtuto a tusdten _____

7 eakt netnsi lsoesns _____

8 ytusd rfo na xmea _____

2 Complete the text with the phrases from Exercise 1.

The Idea Spot

Try something new! Here are a few ideas.

1   <u>Learn to drive</u>   a car. You can learn at MPH Driving School.

2 _____ in Italy!
You can take classes in Milan, Rome, or Florence.

3 Can you play sports? _____
from Ralph Garvis at the Youth Gym.

4 _____ !
Baila has flamenco, tango, and salsa classes.

5 You can _____ .
Use your own computer. Tech Now teaches you online.

6 _____ with a friend.
Go to the library or a café. Get an A on your test!

7 _____ . Students at
Byron Language School need help in Japanese and Chinese. Volunteer today!

8 _____ online.
Find a job as a nurse, doctor, teacher, accountant, musician . . .

3 What are they doing these days? Read the clues and complete the chart with ✓ (yes) or ✗ (no). There is only one answer for each person.

- Carmen is taking a salsa class.
- Thomas isn't working these days.
- Megan isn't learning a language or looking for a job.
- Daniel is taking a language class.

Who is . . .	looking for a job?	taking a dance class?	studying Turkish?	creating a website?
Carmen	✗	✓	✗	✗
Thomas		✗		
Megan		✗		
Daniel		✗		

4 Answer the questions. Use the information in Exercise 3.

1 What's Carmen doing these days? _____

2 What's Thomas doing these days? _____

3 What's Megan doing these days? _____

4 What's Daniel doing these days? _____

5 Match the questions and answers.

1 What class is Debbie taking? ___e___

2 Where is Kathryn going? _____

3 Is Tonya creating a website? _____

4 Are Cindy and Mia tutoring students? _____

5 Why is Anna studying Italian? _____

6 Are you looking for a job? _____

a Because she's looking for a job in Rome.

b Yes, she is.

c She's going to her dance class.

d No, I'm not.

e She's taking a Spanish class.

f No, they're not.

6 Write present continuous questions with the information in parentheses.

1 (What / you / do / these days)   _What are you doing these days_   ?
2 (you / take / an art class)   _____ ?
3 (Brad / take / the class)   _____ ?
4 (Where / you / study / French)   _____ ?
5 (What / you and Dave / do / these days) _____ ?

7 Complete the conversation with the correct questions from Exercise 6.

Erin Hi, Fei. _What are you doing these days_   ?
                        1

Fei   Oh, I'm studying French!

Erin _____ ?
                        2

Fei   At the Bonjour Language School.

Erin _____ ?
                        3

Fei   No, he's not. He's taking tennis lessons.

Erin Tennis? That's great.

Fei   He loves it. So, _____ ?
                              4

Erin We're painting and drawing a lot!

Fei   _____ ?
                        5

Erin Yes, we are! Oh, I'm late. Bye, Fei.

Fei   Bye, Erin. I mean, *au revoir!*

8 What are you doing these days? Answer the questions with your own information.

1 Are you taking any sports lessons?   _____
2 Where are your friends studying English?   _____
3 Is your English teacher studying a language? _____
4 Are you studying for an exam this week?   _____
5 Is your mother or father looking for a job? _____
6 Where are you eating out these days?   _____
7 Is your brother or sister taking guitar lessons? _____
8 What are you reading?   _____

D What's new?

1 Look at the photo in Exercise 2. What are the people doing?

_____

2 Read the text. Write the names.

1 Ron's son: _____

2 Ron's wife: _____

○ ○ ○   Outspring Mail

✉   ✎   ←   ⇄   ↱   ✓   ⊙   ⓘ   ⓘ   🖨   ⊠   ♻   Q▾ All
Get Mail New   Reply Reply All Forward Mark Read Defer   Next Previous Print   Delete Junk   Search

Hey, Jeremy!

How are you? What are you doing these days? I'm finally taking a computer class! I'm
creating my own website. I'm posting a lot of pictures and videos, too. The pictures
are of my kids, of course! Paul's ten now. He's helping me with my website! He's
learning so much about computers at school. After school, he's taking soccer lessons
at the park. His coach is Mr. Gonzalez–who is also tutoring Molly in Spanish! Molly is
twelve, and she's taking tennis lessons. Is your daughter playing sports?

My wife and I are taking a Japanese class. Julie's also studying Spanish, and she's
looking for a job. Are you and Beth cooking at home these days? We love your Greek
salad and chicken! Are you still taking dance classes? Let's all go salsa dancing soon!

Write soon,
Ron

P.S. Here's a photo for you. We're eating sushi at your favorite Japanese restaurant!

---

3 Read the text again. Then answer the questions.

1 Is Ron creating a website?   _Yes, he is._____

2 Who is helping Ron with his website?   _____

3 What sport is Paul learning?   _____

4 Who is tutoring Ron's daughter?   _____

5 Is Ron's wife studying a language?   _____

6 Is Ron's wife working?   _____

Past experiences

A Last weekend

1 Complete the conversations with the correct present continuous forms of the verbs from the box.

| listen | play | play | shop | ✓ stay | stay out | visit | watch |

A. **Alan** Hey, Mike. Where are you?

Mike At home. I'm _____staying_____ home
1

this weekend.

Alan What are you doing?

Mike I'm _____ an old movie.
2

Are you home?

Alan No. I'm _____ relatives.
3

B. **Tomas** Hey, Clara. What are you doing these days?

Clara Oh, I'm _____ in a band!
1

Tomas Really? So are you _____ late
2

on weekends?

Clara Yes! We usually play at 10:00 p.m. What about you?
What are you doing on weekends?

Tomas Oh, I'm _____ basketball on
3

Saturdays and soccer on Sundays. That's all.

Clara Hey, so come to one of our concerts!

C. **Bree** Hi, Yoko. Can you talk right now?

Yoko Yes. I'm just _____ to
1

music. Why?

Bree Oh, I'm _____ for new
2

clothes and I need help.

Yoko OK, I can help you. Where are you?

2 Complete the chart with the correct simple past forms of the verbs from the box.

chat	cry	dance	like	✓ play	shop	study	visit

+ ed	+ d	y → i, + ed	double consonant + ed
played			

3 Look at the calendar. Write sentences about Vincent's activities last week. Use the simple past forms of the verbs.

MONDAY	
morning	exercise with Ray
afternoon	
evening	call Mom

TUESDAY	
morning	
afternoon	work at the bookstore
evening	

WEDNESDAY	
morning	play tennis with Ray
afternoon	
evening	watch videos

THURSDAY	
morning	
afternoon	visit Grandpa
evening	fix Dan's computer

FRIDAY	
morning	
afternoon	study for the test with Lara
evening	shop for a new computer

1   Vincent and Ray exercised on Monday
    morning.
2   Vincent
3
4
5
6
7
8
9

4 Complete Rachel's blog with the correct simple past forms of the verbs in parentheses.

FOLLOW ME!

LAST WEEK

On Monday, my sister and I _____shopped_____ (shop) for new clothes at the mall.
                                        1

I _____ (look for) a green dress for my friend's party. On Tuesday, I
              2

_____ (search) online for green shoes!
        3

I _____ (not / exercise) every day last week, but I _____
              4   5

(exercise) on Tuesday and Thursday.

On Friday, I _____ (listen) to music with Jamie, and we
                         6

_____ (watch) a movie. We _____ (not / watch) a new movie,
        7   8

but an old movie from 1927! The actors _____ (not / talk) in the movie, and it was
                                                     9

in black and white. We _____ (love) the movie! We _____
                              10   11

(laugh) and we _____ (cry).
                          12

5 Write simple past sentences about you, your family, and your friends with the information in parentheses. Use time expressions.

Example: _My brother listened to music last weekend._

1 (listen to music)   _____

2 (stay home)   _____

3 (stay out late)   _____

4 (use social media)   _____

5 (not / exercise)   _____

6 (not / visit relatives) _____

7 (play soccer)   _____

8 (not / play video games) _____

9 (watch a movie)   _____

10 (not / stream music)   _____

B You're kidding!

1 Complete the conversations with the correct words from the boxes.

A. | not | ✓oh | yes | you're kidding |

Leo   I'm studying Japanese.

Amy   _____ *Oh* _____ ?
               1

Leo   _____ , and I'm also studying Korean, Spanish, and Italian.
               2

Amy   _____ !
               3

Leo   No. I'm _____ . And I'm taking Chinese!
                       4

B. | know | oh, yeah | what | yes |

Chris   I have an English test on Tuesday.

Paul   _____ ?
               1

Chris   _____ , and I didn't study.
               2

Paul   _____ ? You always study on weekends.
               3

Chris   I _____ , but I played soccer all weekend!
               4

C. | at | for | really | yeah |

Ellie   I shopped for new clothes last weekend.

Pat   _____ ? Where?
               1

Ellie   _____ the mall. And now I have a new suit.
               2

Pat   _____ ? You always wear T-shirts and jeans.
               3

Ellie   I know, but I'm looking _____ a job, and I have an interview.
                               4

2 Match the conversations in Exercise 1 with the pictures.

1 ☐   2 ☐   3 ☐

C Did you make dinner last night?

1 Circle the verbs that complete both expressions.

1 (have) / do: a party   a car
2 see / go: to work   grocery shopping
3 go / **make**:   breakfast   dinner
4 get / **make**:   a haircut   a job
5 go / **see**:   friends   a play
6 **make** / do: the dishes   laundry

2 Complete the conversations with some of the expressions from Exercise 1.
Use the present continuous forms of the verbs.

1   **A**   What are you doing?
     B   _I'm doing laundry._

2   **A**   Do you have a minute?
     B   I can't talk right now.
        _____ .

3   **A**   Hi, Eva. Is this a good time?
     B   I'm sorry. _____
        _____ right now.

4   **A**   Can you talk?
     B   I'm busy right now.
        _____ .

5   **A**   What are you doing, Dan?
     B   _____ .

6   **A**   Can you help me with
        my computer?
     B   Sorry, Mom. _____
        _____ .

3 Circle the correct words to complete the conversations.

1 **A** _____ she get a haircut?

   B No, she didn't.

     a Does

     (b) Did

     c Do

2 **A** Did you do laundry yesterday?

   B _____

     a Yes, I do.

     b Yes, I did.

     c Yes, I didn't.

3 **A** Did you see Carol on Friday?

   B No, I didn't. I _____ Wendy.

     a see

     b seed

     c saw

4 **A** Did Todd ride a bike to work?

   B No, he didn't. He _____ .

     a didn't drive

     b drove

     c drives

5 **A** Did they _____ some water at the park?

   B No, they didn't.

     a drink

     b drank

     c drinked

6 **A** Did you eat pizza at the restaurant?

   B No, we didn't. We _____ tacos.

     a eat

     b ate

     c eated

4 Write simple past *yes* / *no* questions about the information in the sentences. Then answer the questions with short answers.

1 Sue bought new clothes at the mall.

   A _Did Sue buy new clothes at the mall_ ?

   B _Yes, she did_ .

2 Ethan and Craig took a bus to Miami.

   A _____ ?

   B No, _____ .

3 He did the dishes last night.

   A _____ ?

   B No, _____ .

4 They went to work on Friday.

   A _____ ?

   B Yes, _____ .

5 **Complete the text with the correct simple past forms of the verbs in parentheses.**

David _____had_____ (have) a bad day
                    1

yesterday. He _____ (get up) late,
                        2

so he _____ (not / make) breakfast.
              3

He _____ (run) to the bus stop,
          4

but he _____ (see) the bus drive
              5

away. He _____ (take) a taxi to work,
                6

and he _____ (get) to work late. He
              7

_____ (sit) at his desk and looked
          8

at his computer. He _____ (read) the
                              9

note for Monday: "Martin Luther King Day. No work."

David _____ (go) home, and he
              10

_____ (sleep) for three hours.
          11

6 **Answer the questions with the information from Exercise 5.**

1   Did David get up late?   _Yes, he did._____

2   Did David make breakfast?   _____

3   Did David take a bus to work?   _____

4   Did David get to work late?   _____

5   Did David work yesterday?   _____

7 **Check (✓) the things you did last week. Then write sentences about what you did and didn't do.**

1   ☐   get up late   _____

2   ☐   do laundry   _____

3   ☐   buy new clothes   _____

4   ☐   meet a friend   _____

5   ☐   go to a play   _____

6   ☐   get a haircut   _____

7   ☐   read a book   _____

8   ☐   eat at a restaurant   _____

D I saw a great movie.

1 Read the text. Then circle the correct answers.

1 Jeremy went to _____ .

  a Mexico   b Ohio   c China

2 He went with _____ .

  a Beth and Ron   b Beth and Ron's daughter   c Beth and Brittany

3 He saw _____ .

  a his friends   b his parents   c Ron

Hi, Ron,

We're on vacation in Sandusky, Ohio!

This vacation is all about our daughter, Brittany! We came to Ohio for Cedar Point. It's a great amusement park. We're staying with friends. They have a daughter, too. We went to Cedar Point on Tuesday. Thursday we went to Cedar Point Shores. It's a water park. Brittany had a great time.

Beth and I are having fun, too. We liked Cedar Point and Cedar Point Shores. Last night we saw a play. We aren't cooking at all! We had dinner at a Mexican restaurant and a Chinese restaurant. We're eating at a lot of cafés, too.

Right now we're relaxing—and writing postcards!

Jeremy

2 Read the text again. Correct the false sentences.

1 Jeremy and his family went to Cedar, Ohio.

  <u>Jeremy and his family went to Sandusky, Ohio.</u>

2 Jeremy and his family are staying with relatives.

  _____

3 Jeremy and his family went to the amusement park on Wednesday.

  _____

4 Jeremy and Beth liked Cedar Point, but they didn't like Cedar Point Shores.

  _____

5 Jeremy and Beth saw a movie last night.

  _____

6 On their vacation, Jeremy and his family didn't eat out.

  _____

Getting away

A Where were you?

1 Complete the puzzle with the correct adjectives.

Across

3 This is a _____ party. We're having a great time.

5 Those hot dogs were _____ . I didn't eat them.

6 I went to an _____ soccer game last weekend! The players were very good.

8 This game is _____ . It's 0 to 0, and my favorite player isn't playing.

Down

1 That was an _____ book. I read it in 2015 and again this year.

2 Can we watch a different movie? This is _____ !

4 The library is always _____ .

7 My brother's friends are very _____ . I can't study!

9 This food isn't great, but it's not bad. It's _____ .

					1 I			2	
		3			N				
					T	4			
					E				
		5			R				
					E				
					S				
					T				
	6				I		7		
					N				
8	9				G				

2 What do you think? Label the pictures with two possible adjectives from Exercise 1.

1 ___exciting___
___noisy___

2 _____
_____

3 _____
_____

4 _____
_____

5 _____
_____

3 Put the words in the correct order to make sentences.

1 class / Lola / Was / in / Monday morning / on / ? _Was Lola in class on Monday morning?_

2 an / they / yesterday / amusement park / Were / at / ? _____

3 a / at / We / museum / were / . _____

4 was / fun and exciting / It / . _____

5 were / , / Yes / they / . _____

6 weekend / Jim's / How / was / ? _____

7 she / No / , / wasn't / . _____

8 you and Chris / on / Where / were / Friday afternoon / ? _____

4 Label the pictures with the correct questions and answers from Exercise 3.

1 _Was Lola in class on Monday morning_ ?   2 _____ ?

_____ .   _____ .

3 _____ ?   4 _____ ?

_____ .   _____ .

82

5 Complete the text with the correct forms of the simple past of *be (not)*.

Did you read a good book?
TELL US WHAT YOU THINK!

Gwennie

I read Moby Dick. It _____was_____ boring.
1

I didn't like it.

Dan91

No . . . Moby Dick _____ boring!
2

It _____ interesting! I loved it.
3

LukeMan

Wow, Dan91! You're kidding, right? Moby Dick _____
4

interesting at all! It's 822 pages!

KatyG

OK, long, yes, but boring, no! Moby Dick _____ exciting. I
5

read four Herman Melville books, and they _____ all great!
6

TylerT

What? I don't think so. I read three of his books, and they

_____ great. They _____ all terrible!
7   8

6 Answer the questions with your own information.

1 How was your weekend?   _____

2 Where were you in 2017?   _____

3 How old were you in 2015?   _____

4 Was your last vacation interesting?   _____

5 Were you in English class yesterday?   _____

6 Where were you on Monday?   _____

7 Where were your parents last night?   _____

8 Were you and a friend at a concert last week?   _____

B That's great!

1 Read the news. Is it good or bad? Write G (good news) or B (bad news).

1 I got a promotion. I'm so happy! _G_

2 I missed my flight. Now I'm waiting for the next flight. _____

3 I was sick yesterday. My friends saw a great play without me. _____

4 I won a contest and got a trip to Mexico. It's so exciting! _____

5 I lost my new cell phone. I bought it last week, and it was $800! _____

6 I got a new job. It's very interesting! _____

2 Write the conversation in the correct order.

> ✓ Did you have a good weekend?
>
> It was great. I went to a new club with friends.
>
> It was OK. I stayed home all weekend. I was sick.
>
> Thanks. And how was your weekend?
>
> That's nice!
>
> That's too bad.

A _Did you have a good weekend?_ _____

B _It was OK._ _____

A _____

B _____

A _____

B _____

3 Write a conversation with some of the sentences from the box. Use the conversation in Exercise 2 as a model.

| It was good. I saw an interesting play. | Oh, no! | That's awesome! |
| It wasn't great. I lost my wallet. | That's excellent! | That's terrible! |

A _Did you have a good weekend?_ _____

B _____

A _____

B _____

A _____

B _____

C My vacation

1 Complete the sentences with vacation activities. Use the simple past forms of the verbs.

1 Tim s<u>hopped</u> in m<u>arkets</u>
  and b_____
  s_____ in Tokyo.

2 Donna w_____
  to a f_____
  in Cuzco.

3 Eric w_____ to
  the b_____ and
  r_____ in Rio.

4 Tina t_____
  p_____ of the
  Eiffel Tower in Paris.

5 Laura t_____ a
  t_____ of the Taj
  Mahal in Agra.

6 Rick and Lisa w_____
  s_____ in San
  Francisco.

2 Cross out the words that don't make phrases with the verbs.

1 **go:**	to the beach	~~pictures~~	sightseeing
2 **take:**	a tour	to a festival	pictures
3 **relax:**	souvenirs	at home	at a hotel
4 **buy:**	new clothes	souvenirs	sightseeing
5 **shop:**	in a market	online	a tour

3 Look at the tour information. Then answer the questions in full sentences.

MEREDITH**TRAVEL** TOURS   MIAMI, FLORIDA

Last name	First name	Day	People traveling with	Getting to Miami by	Activities	Time
Arai	Hiro	Monday	wife	train	go sightseeing	11:00 a.m.– 9:00 p.m.
Clark	Patty	Tuesday	–	train	take a tour of the Frost Museum of Science	10:00 a.m.– 12:00 p.m.
Hall	Lucy	Thursday	husband, two children	car	go to Zoo Miami	8:00 a.m.– 8:00 p.m.
Vargas	Ricardo	Wednesday	wife, one child	bus	go to the Seaquarium	9:00 a.m.– 4:00 p.m.
Young	Harry	Tuesday	–	bus	go to an art festival	2:00 p.m.– 6:00 p.m.

1 Where did Patty go on vacation? _She went to Miami._

2 What did Hiro and his wife do in Miami? _____

3 Who did Lucy travel with? _____

4 How did Harry get to Miami? _____

5 What time did Patty's tour start? _____

6 How did Ricardo and his family get to Miami? _____

7 What time did the art festival end? _____

8 What did Ricardo and his family do in Miami? _____

4 Read the answers. Write the *Wh-* questions for the underlined part of the answers.
Use the information from Exercise 3.

1 _How did Lucy and her family get to Miami?_ They drove.

2 _____ He traveled with <u>his wife and child</u>.

3 _____ She <u>took a tour of the Frost Museum of Science</u>.

4 _____ He went to the art festival <u>on Tuesday</u>.

5 _____ They <u>took a train</u>.

6 _____ It started at <u>2:00 p.m.</u>

5 Complete the conversation with simple past *Wh-* questions.

Holly Hi, Grace. <u>How was your vacation</u>?
1

Grace My vacation was great.

Holly _____?
2

Grace I went to Costa Rica!

Holly That's exciting! _____?
3

Grace My brother and our friends Doug and Kim.

Holly That's nice. _____?
4

Grace We flew. We left at 6:00 a.m. We flew to Miami and then to San José.

Holly _____?
5

Grace We got to San José at 4:30.

Holly Oh, that's not bad. _____?
6

Grace We went sightseeing in San José, and then we went to the beach for four days and relaxed!

Holly Awesome! _____?
7

Grace Oh, the food was excellent. We ate a lot.

6 Think about the last time you visited relatives or friends in another city or country. Answer the questions.

1 Where did you go? _____

2 How old were you? _____

3 Who did you see? _____

4 Who did you travel with? _____

5 How did you get there? _____

6 What did you do there? _____

7 What did you eat there? _____

8 What did you buy there? _____

9 Did you get up early or late? _____

10 Was it exciting or boring? _____

D Travel experiences

1 Label the pictures with the correct headings from the text in Exercise 2.

1 _Make a Schedule_   2 _____   3 _____   4 _____

2 Read the text. Then answer the questions.

✈ TRAVEL TIPS

Be safe when you travel. Here are some things you can do to have a fun vacation. Learn from our readers' mistakes!

GET A HOTEL
Plan your trip before you go! Leo took a bus to Salvador in Brazil. He didn't get a hotel before the trip. When he got to Salvador, he didn't find a hotel at first. He finally found one, but he paid a lot of money for it!

CHECK THE WEATHER
Learn about the weather before your trip. Rachel went to Rome, but she didn't check the weather for Italy. She took only T-shirts and shorts, and she didn't take a coat. Brrrrrrr! She was cold.

MAKE A SCHEDULE
Write down the days of your trip, and make a list of things to do each day. Ken and Lee went to South Korea, but they didn't make a list. The first two days of their trip were wasted. They didn't do anything fun because they didn't know where to go. They finally went sightseeing in Seoul, but they didn't go to the markets. They bought souvenirs at the airport!

REMEMBER YOUR WALLET
Don't forget your wallet and passport. Margot got to the airport for her trip to Sydney, Australia. Her wallet and her passport were at home. She missed her flight!

1 How did Leo get to Salvador?   _He took a bus._

2 What clothes did Rachel take to Rome?   _____

3 Who did Ken travel with?   _____

4 Did Ken buy souvenirs at the markets in Seoul? _____

5 Where was Margot's wallet?   _____

Time to celebrate

A I'm going to get married.

1 Complete the sequences with the correct months.

1 January   March   _____May_____   July

2 _____   July   August   September

3 September   October   November   _____

4 January   _____   July   October

5 _____   May   August   November

2 Look at Kelly's birthday calendar. When is each person's birthday?
Write sentences with words for the dates.

Birthday Calendar

Sort by: date

Makoto Saito
June 22nd

Kyle Brown
June 23rd

Lucia Ferrari
June 29th

Jack O'Dell
June 30th

Don Stuart
July 1st

Daniel Lucas
July 5th

Amanda Rivera
July 8th

Emily Simpson
July 12th

1 _Makoto's birthday is June_
   twenty-second.

2 _____
   _____

3 _____
   _____

4 _____

5 _____

6 _____

7 _____

8 _____
   _____

3 Circle the correct words to complete each sentence.

1 Jacob's **going to** / **go to** visit relatives on Sunday.

2 Mr. and Mrs. Davis **are going drive** / **are going to drive** to work next week.

3 We're **are not going to** / **not going to** go to the beach.

4 Chet **is going to not take** / **isn't going to take** the train to work.

5 **A** Are you **going to stay** / **go to staying** home today?

   B Yes, **I am going** / **I am**.

6 **A** **Is Sarah go** / **Is Sarah going** to study in Brazil?

   B No, **she isn't** / **she doesn't**.

4 Look at the calendar. Write sentences about the people's future plans with *be going to*.
Use the words in parentheses.

January	February	March
		22 – Ellie's trip to Ecuador

April	May	June
21 – Dana's 1st day at new job	7 – Tim's graduation from college	2 – Willy's vacation (one week)

July	August	September
23 – Jill and Lucas go skydiving!		10 – Brian and Nicole's 1st day of college

October	November	December
11 – Amy and Ken's wedding		13 – Heather's big party

1 (travel)   Ellie is going to travel to Ecuador on March 22nd.

2 (start her new job)   _____

3 (graduate from college) _____

4 (go on vacation)   _____

5 (go skydiving)   _____

6 (start college)   _____

7 (get married)   _____

8 (have a party)   _____

5 Write *yes / no* questions with *be going to* and the information in parentheses.
Then complete the answers.

1 (you / take / a taxi / to work)

A ___Are you going to take a taxi to work___ ?

B Yes, ___I am___ .

2 (they / get / married / next week)

A _____ ?

B No, _____ .

3 (he / create / a website for me)

A _____ ?

B No, _____ .

4 (we / eat out / on Friday)

A _____ ?

B Yes, _____ .

5 (she / look for / a job)

A _____ ?

B Yes, _____ .

6 (you / do / the dishes / tonight)

A _____ ?

B No, _____ .

6 Complete the chart with information about future plans for you, your family,
or your friends. Use the events in the box or your own ideas.

| get married | graduate | start a new job |
| go skydiving | have a big party | travel to [country name] |

	Person	Event	Date
Example:	Max and Leah	get married	August 3rd
1			
2			
3			
4			
5			
6			

7 Write sentences with the information in Exercise 6 and *be going to*.

Example: ___Max and Leah are going to get married on___
___August 3rd.___

1 _____

2 _____

3 _____

4 _____

5 _____

6 _____

B Sure. I'd love to.

1 Complete the words with the correct letters.

Declining an invitation	Accepting an invitation
1 I'm s<u>orry</u>_____ . I can't.	4 S_____ . I'd l_____ to.
2 I'm a_____ I can't.	5 Yeah. That s_____ gr_____ .
3 I'm r_____ sorry, but I can't.	6 S_____ go_____ .

2 Complete the conversation with phrases from Exercise 1. More than one answer is possible.

Sam Hello?

Ty Hi, Sam. It's Ty. Listen, do you want to go to a basketball game on Saturday?

Sam Saturday? _____ .
                                    1

Ty Oh, OK. Well, do you want to go to the beach on Sunday?

Sam The beach? _____ .
                                       2

Ty Great. I'm going to drive. Can we meet at your house at 9:00 a.m.?

Sam _____ ! See you at
                              3
9:00 on Sunday.

3 Write a conversation about invitations with the phrases from Exercise 1 and your own ideas. Use the conversation in Exercise 2 as a model.

Marc Hello?

Dina _____

Marc _____

Dina _____

Marc _____

Dina _____

Marc _____

Planning a party

1 **Put the letters in the correct order to make party checklist phrases.**

1 hosoce het uscmi _____choose the music_____

2 dsen het osiivtnitan _____

3 mkea a eusgt slti _____

4 lpan eht mneu _____

5 kabe a ceka _____

6 tedaeroc eth omor _____

7 ybu a fgit _____

8 ppeerra hte dofo _____

2 **Look at the pictures. Complete the sentences with the phrases from Exercise 1 and *be going to*.**

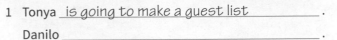

1 Tonya _is going to make a guest list_ .

Danilo _____ .

2 Ben _____ .

Mi Yon _____ .

3 Glenn _____ .

Terry _____ .

4 Rodrigo _____ .

Erica _____ .

3 Complete the chart with the correct object pronouns.

Subject pronouns:	I	you	he	she	it	we	they
Object pronouns:	me						

4 Rewrite the email to correct the underlined mistakes.

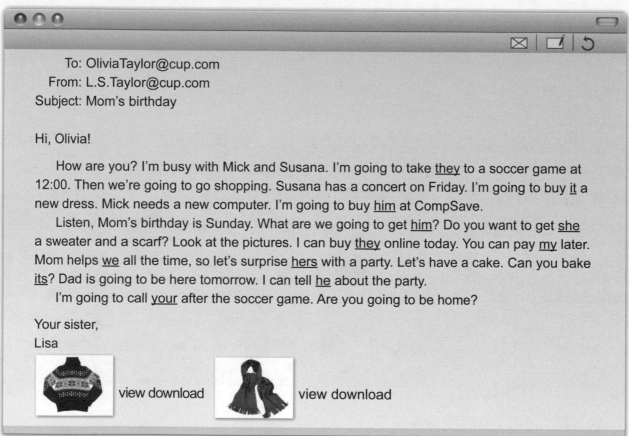

To: OliviaTaylor@cup.com
From: L.S.Taylor@cup.com
Subject: Mom's birthday

Hi, Olivia!

How are you? I'm busy with Mick and Susana. I'm going to take <u>they</u> to a soccer game at 12:00. Then we're going to go shopping. Susana has a concert on Friday. I'm going to buy <u>it</u> a new dress. Mick needs a new computer. I'm going to buy <u>him</u> at CompSave.

Listen, Mom's birthday is Sunday. What are we going to get <u>him</u>? Do you want to get <u>she</u> a sweater and a scarf? Look at the pictures. I can buy <u>they</u> online today. You can pay <u>my</u> later. Mom helps <u>we</u> all the time, so let's surprise <u>hers</u> with a party. Let's have a cake. Can you bake <u>its</u>? Dad is going to be here tomorrow. I can tell <u>he</u> about the party.

I'm going to call <u>your</u> after the soccer game. Are you going to be home?

Your sister,
Lisa

view download   view download

How are you? I'm busy with Mick and Susana. I'm going to take them to a
soccer game at 12:00.

_____

_____

_____

_____

_____

_____

_____

5 **Put the words in the correct order to make sentences.**

1 going / to / buy / you / What / are / Jen / ?   <u>What are you going to buy Jen?</u>
2 help / going / Henry and me / Who's / to / ?   _____
3 John / going / When / to / you / are / see / ?   _____
4 to / is / going / How / Sonya / send / the invitations / ?   _____
5 to / What time / Paul and Vera / going / is / he / call / ?   _____
6 is / Where / going / she / meet / to / you and Jim / ?   _____

6 **Write conversations with the questions from Exercise 5 and the information in the pictures.**
Use object pronouns in the answers.

1 **A**   <u>What are you going to buy Jen?</u>
   B   <u>I'm going to buy her a hat.</u>

What: Lilly's birthday party
When: Friday, May 4th
Where: At Kate's house

SEND

2 **A**   _____
   B   _____

3 **A**   _____
   B   _____

4 **A**   _____
   B   _____

5 **A**   _____
   B   _____

6 **A**   _____
   B   _____

D Birthdays

1 Look at the invitation. What are they going to celebrate?

_____

Celebrate!

Host: Kelly
What: A party for Joe's birthday!
Where: Kelly's house
542 Maple Street
When: Saturday, June 14th
6:00 p.m.

It's Joe's birthday. Let's give him a great party! Shhh . . . don't tell him! I'm going to prepare dinner and bake a cake. Come early and help me decorate the house! Bring him a gift or a card. Are you going to come? Don't be late!

Are you going to come?

◯ **Yes** ◯ **No**

Guests: [_____]

Post a comment:

[_____]

● Yes

RayS: Sure. I'm going to come!
Matt Blake: It sounds great. I'm going to bring my wife.
Dawn447: Josh and I are going to be there. See you on Saturday.
Ellie Smith: I'm going to bring my guitar and play him a song!
Paul Peters: I'm going to be late, but I'm going to be there!

● No

Lydia: I'm sorry, I can't. My mother is visiting, and we are going to see a play that night.
Ali: I'm afraid I can't come to Joe's party. Tell him "Happy Birthday!"

2 Read the invitation again. Then write T (true), F (false), or NI (no information).

1 The party is at 6:00 p.m. on June 14th. ___T___

2 Guests are going to dance at the party. _____

3 Kelly is going to bake a cake. _____

4 Matt's wife isn't going to come to the party. _____

5 Ellie can play the guitar. _____

6 Lydia is going to buy Joe a gift. _____